Zakynthos

Travel Guide

Quick Trips Series

Table of Contents

Zakynthos (Zante)

The lovely Greek island of Zakynthos (also known by its Italian name, Zante) has a reputation for fun and is one of the country's most popular holiday islands. Zante is the third-largest island in the Ionian Sea just off Greece's west coast.

ZAKYNTHOS TRAVEL GUIDE

Homer refers to the island in his works the Iliad and Odyssey, stating that Zakynthos, a prince of Troy and son of King Dardanos arrived here between 1500 and 1600 BC. The Italians named it Zacinto and in more recent years, following the struggle for national independence, it became Zante.

One of Zante's main attractions is arranged by mother nature. Every year loggerhead turtles descend upon the Bay of Laganas in Zante to nest. The wonder of young hatchlings bravely venturing towards the sea is beautiful and miraculous, and draws a fair amount of tourists.

The invitingly azure waters draw human visitors to Zante as well. The coastline alternates between craggy rock features and golden, sandy beaches. The East Coast of the island has numerous small coves that are ideal for snorkelling and underwater exploration. The West Coast

offers amazing cliffside views and beautifully painted

sunset skies. The island is also unusually fertile. Olive

groves are found everywhere and a variety of fruits and

vegetables are cultivated here. Not everyone, though,

seeks holiday fun by daylight and the flipside of Zante's

allure is the vibrant party atmosphere that often lasts until

sunrise.

🌏 Customs & Culture

The Venetians have left an indelible imprint on the island

of Zante during their years of occupation, particularly in

the expression of art and literature. Ionian painting

enjoyed a brief spell of prominence throughout Greece in

the 17th century, particularly thanks to artists such as

Panagiotis Doxaras. Zante has given birth to several

poets, novelists and composers, including Dionysios

Solomos, who wrote the words to the Greek national anthem.

The Greek Orthodox faith dominates in the Greek islands, accounting for roughly 98 percent of the population. There are minorities of Jews, Catholics and Muslims. Family values are important and islands are proud of their Greek nationality. Insulting the Greek Orthodox Church or the Greek nation may generate a bad reaction with the locals, but otherwise, the people of Zante are friendly, laid-back and tolerant of foreign tourists. Although the official language is Greek, English is widely spoken.

Music plays an important role in Zante's culture. Singing and dancing are an important component of festivals on Zakynthos and the guitar and mandolin are commonly played. A traditional form is the "Kandatha", in which improvised lyrics is sung to the accompaniment of mandolin and guitar. The earliest forms of Greek opera originated here and it is the site of the first music school in Greece. The first Philharmonic Orchestra was founded in 1816. Nowadays other forms of musical expression take precedence. Zante hosts an annual jazz festival, but it is the island's nightclub scene that is well known across Europe.

The cuisine is another highlight of Zante. Olives and Honey are cultivated in a variety of places and enjoyed in the food of its restaurants and taverns. Nougat is one speciality of Zakynthos. Other traditional favorites are pastreli and fritoures.

🌐 Geography

Zante belongs to the Ionian Islands of Greece. It is third largest and also the southern most of the group, which consists of seven islands. The island has a permanent population of about 35,000 people and covers 405 square km. It is about 300km west of Athens and has a coastline of 123km. It is 20km west of Peloponnese on the mainland and 15km north of the island Kefalonia. The highest point is Vrachionas, which rises to a height of 758m. Its currency is the euro.

During peak holiday season, Zante is linked to a number of cities via direct flights, but from November to April, visitors have to travel via Athens. As Zante is a popular destination with Italian tourists, a regular ferry service connects with the Italian harbors of Venice, Trieste, Ancona, Bari and Brindisi. The island has two ports. While most water traffic passes through the port at Zante Town, the ferry to Kefalonia departs from the port at Agios Nikolaos. The island has a bus service, but this does not operate over weekends. Other options for transport are taxis or car rental.

🌎 Weather & Best Time to Visit

Zante enjoys a Mediterranean climate with hot, dry summers and mild, wet winter months. The most popular holiday season on Zante is from 1 May to 31 October. Outside this period there are no direct flights to the island and visitors have to travel via Athens.

July and August are the hottest months when temperatures might rise as high as 40 degrees Celsius. For these months, the average day temperature is 31 degrees Celsius, with average night temperatures between 20 and 21 degrees Celsius. In August, humidity increases. June and September see average day temperatures around 28 degrees Celsius, with May and October recording averages of between 23 and 24 degrees Celsius. Average day temperatures between December and March will hover from 14 to 16 degrees Celsius, while November and April see average day temperatures around 19 degrees Celsius. Night temperatures between 8 and 9 degrees Celsius occur between the months of December and March. October, November, April and May see night temperatures that fall in the mid-teens.

In May, there are fewer tourists, plenty of spring flowers and warm days to enjoy. The evenings are perhaps a little cooler. September is another month when the beaches and other facilities are less crowded with holidaymakers.

ZAKYNTHOS TRAVEL GUIDE

The weather remains mostly pleasant, although a few rainy days may be experienced. Rain can be expected to occur more regularly between October and February.

Sights & Activities: What to See & Do

🌐 Zante Town

Zante Town is often referred to as the Venice of the

South. It features a blend of Byzantine and Venetian

architecture, with some English and French influences

added. A damaging earthquake, followed by a major fire,

wreaked much destruction in the capital, but some of the

traditional Venetian arches and picturesque squares that the city was famous for, have been preserved.

In Zante Town, you will find the church of St Dionysios. Several churches on the island are associated with St Dionysios, who is the patron saint of both Zakynthos and fishermen, but the one located near the port of the capital is the largest. Although from a noble family, the Sigouros of Zakynthos, the saint was known for his humility and spirituality. He was born in 1547 in the village of Aigialos, on Zakynthos. The church, however, was erected only in 1948.

Several of the city's attractions are located around Solomos or St Marco Square. The main shopping district can be found along Alexandre Roma Street and its surroundings. Its busiest street is Strata Marina, which leads to the port. As the capital, it is also the commercial heart of the island.

Solomos Square

Dionysios Solomos was born on Zante or Zakynthos in 1798. He is best known throughout Greece as the poet who wrote Hymn to Liberty in 1923. The first two stanzas of this, later became the Greek National anthem, but his influence on Greek poetry does not end there. Through the study and preservation of older forms of poetry he effectively forged a bridge between Old and Modern styles, illustrating that the one cannot exist without the other. Besides Hymn to Liberty, very little of his work was published before he died. While the poem did achieve acclaim for its creator, the legacy of Dionysios Solomos is best appreciated in hindsight.

ZAKYNTHOS TRAVEL GUIDE

Solomos Square, the larger and most central square of Zante Town is named after the poet. It is flanked by important sights such as the Byzantine Museum of Zakynthos, the Church of St Nikolaos on the Mole and the Cultural Center of Zakynthos. The key feature of the square is a statue of the poet Dionysios Solomos, after whom it had been named. Solomos was the Greek National Poet and is famous for having penned the Greek National Anthem. The original statue was the work of a sculptor from Athens, Georgios Vroukos, but a replica has in recent times replaced this. There are several other statues, among them the statue of freedom, and statues to pay tribute to Ugo Foskolo, the Italian poet born on Zante and Pavlos Karer. The square was previously known as Port Square, since it is located at the end of the Central Port of Zante Town.

Byzantine Museum

Zante Town

Tel: +30 26950 42714

The Zakynthos Museum of Byzantine and Post-Byzantine Art was founded in 1960 and hosts a collection that is spread across three levels. It features art from the 12th to 18th century and includes the works of Zakynthian artists such as Damaskinos, Doxaras, Kandounis, Koutouzis, Kantouni and Tzanes. In the first two rooms, various Byzantine icons carved from wood are displayed. The next rooms exhibit original frescoes from the 15th to 17th century. The museum includes a presentation of what the city of Zante Town looked like before the earthquake of 1953 struck.

Museum of Solomos & Kalvos

15 St Marco Square, Zante Town

Tel: +30 26950 28982

http://www.museumsolomos.gr

The Museum of Solomos and Kalvos was founded in 1959, and is located in St Marco Square. It is dedicated to two poets of national importance in Greece. They are Dionysios Solomos and Andreas Kalvos. The building contains the tomb of Solomos and also houses his personal belongings.

The mortal remains of Andreas Kalvos and his wife are also contained within the Mausoleum on the ground floor of the building. The collection features a variety of objects and artefacts. These include pottery, wood carvings, jewellery, crochet and knitted handicrafts, musical instrument, the clothing and weaponry of noble families, furniture, photographs, portraits, sculptures and other works of art dating back to the 18th and 19th century. The Venetian period is well represented and there are items associated with other famous figures from the past of Zakynthos, such as Gregorios Xenopoulos, Ioannis Tsakasianos, the composers Nikolaos Mantzaros and Pavlos Karreris, as well as Dionysios Romas. Admission to the museum is €4. There is another Museum in Zante Town devoted exclusively to the novelist and play writer Gregorios Xenopoulos. This museum is situated near the Church of Agios Dionysios and displays manuscripts as well as other artefacts from his long career.

Venetian Castle

The Venetian castle is located in Bochali, above Zante Town. Allegedly built around 1480, the castle was destroyed when the Turks invaded. Later it was restored under Venetian supervision, but subsequent earthquakes resulted in fresh damage. The castle was constructed over the remains of the Acropolis and features a sculpted crest of the St Marko's lion associated with Venice above its entrance. What remains of the walls and cannons hint at past strength and archaeological excavations have uncovered 12th century structures from the Byzantine era. The site, now tranquil parkland, offers a unique glimpse into the past of Zante.

Mansion of the Roma Family

19 Louka Karer Street

Tel: +30 26950 28381

ZAKYNTHOS TRAVEL GUIDE

The Roma family mansion is one of the very few structures in Zante Town that withstood the earthquake of 1953 with minimal damage and serves as a unique example of the island's architecture before the calamity. The building dates back to 1660, when it was constructed to accommodate Robert John Geoffrey, the Vice Consul of England in Zante.

During the period of English Protection, which lasted from 1816 to 1864, it was called 'Residenza' and served as Seat of the English Resident of Zante. Alexander Roma, of the patriotic military grouping, the 'Greek Red Shirts', acquired the building in 1880. A large number of portraits and other works of art are exhibited within and the libraries contain rare editions of various manuscripts.

Vertzagio Folk Museum

The Vertzagio Folk Museum is basically the reconstruction of a traditional house to demonstrate the Greek lifestyle two hundred years ago. It is located in the Pigadakia Village, which is about 2km from Alykes. A bedroom, living room, dining room and kitchen have been furnished and fully equipped with the tools of the past. Money, linen, newspapers and school desks from the period are displayed. One of the more impressive exhibits is a fully functional grind, once used to press grapes and olives to produce wine and oil respectively.

🌏 Laganas

The Bay of Laganas is shaped by two parallel promontories, both lush and mountainous, that reach to the sea. The town Laganas is reckoned to be the busiest resort town on Zante and it is characterized by a relentless quest for pleasure. The village was developed as a Club 18-30 destination, and features a variety of nightclubs. Accommodation is mainly apartments, rather than hotels. Laganas is popular with young holidaymakers from Germany, the Netherlands, Serbia and the United Kingdom and sometimes the nighttime fun borders on the outrageous. Bars and nightclubs stay open till very late and a variety of tastes are catered for. A large portion of Laganas has been declared a National Park, to protect the turtles that nest here. The area is protected.

National Marine Park

The National Marine Park of Zakynthos was founded in 1999 to afford protection to the loggerhead turtles that nest each year in the Bay of Laganas. It comprises six beaches, namely Gerakas, Daphni, Sekania, Kalamaki, Laganas, and an islet Marathonissi as well as the wetland surrounding Keri Lake and two islands of Strofadia, which are located 50km south of Zakynthos. In the season, the greatest density of turtles are usually found on Sekania, but the whole area can see up to 1800 nests per year, each containing up to 100 eggs.

When adult, loggerhead turtles weigh around 100kg. The females come ashore in the period between June and August, favoring sandy coves for their nests. Although the beaches are open to the public, there are certain restrictions to their use, such as the prohibition of motorized water sports and fishing. Since the turtles tend to come ashore after dark, it is forbidden to visit the above-mentioned beaches after sunset. There has in recent years been some concern that bright lights and excessive noise may interfere with the breeding cycle of the loggerhead turtles.

In the town of Dafni, you will find the Exhibition Center of the National Marine Park. This features a range of exhibits and multimedia that inform on the activities of the Caretta Caretta or loggerhead turtle. Other indigenous fauna and flora are also included.

⊕ Tsilivi

After Laganas, Tsilivi is one of the best-developed resort towns, with an extensive entertainment area of bars and restaurants. The beach is safe, with tranquil, shallow waters and it offers facilities for jet skiing and paragliding. Other attractions are the fantasy mini-golf course, with a number of creative obstacles and the Splash Water Park. The village has become a favorite with all ages.

Tsilivi Waterpark

http://www.tsiliviwaterpark.gr

Opened in 2010, the Tsilivi Waterpark is an initiative of the Xenos Hotel group. The facility has something for all age groups. The children's section includes a number of water-spouting toys, such as dolphins, elephants, mushrooms and octopus. There is the exciting Turbulence slide, for adventurous visitors, as well as the Black Hole and the Space Hole and a Multi-slide. Other features include a Rafting section, a stretch of Lazy River, sunbathing loungers, an Aqua Jungle, a Pirate Boat, the Pools bar and the Restaurant. The grounds are well maintained. The full entry ticket, which is valid for the whole day and includes a free meal, costs €14. The half day ticket is covers entry after 2.30pm and costs €7.

Lockers can be rented for €3, plus a refundable deposit of €5. There is a similar attraction, known as Water Village, in the nearby town, Sarakinado.

Water Village

Sarakinado

Tel: +30 26950 65150

http://www.zantewatervillage.gr/

The summer months in Zante can get quite hot, but fortunately Water Village provides an excellent opportunity to cool down. Located in the village of Sarakinado, just 4km from Zante Town.

The slides and swimming pools vary in size and both children and adults are catered for. Those who want to just relax or chill, may want to settle in the lazy river or in the large size Jacuzzi of the reception pool. Here you can enjoy a drink or just take occupation of one of the sun beds.

At the other extreme, the Boomerbowl tower features a 17m drop followed by a blood-rushing ascent up a near-vertical wall, while the Freefall, the Kamikaze and the High-speed Hydrotube will send you on fast flowing rides of over 70m. Family groups may enjoy the Multi-Racing Slides or the Family Rafting Route. Then there is the Giant Black Hole, which is full of surprises. A full day ticket is €18 for adults. The facility also has various food stands and booth where you can buy souvenir photographs. If you think you might want to come back several times, you could consider purchasing a season pass for €50.

🌐 Argassi

The beach at Argassi is long, but narrow and offers facilities for various water sports. The center of town is vibrant and lively, but it is possible to enjoy a little tranquillity on its outskirts. If you are looking for a little more quiet and a typically Greek atmosphere, consider nearby Kalamaki. A striking and distinctive feature of the coastline of Argassi, is an Old Bridge, dating back to 1885, that now stands submerged in water. At one time, this bridge was part of the main road, which erosion has caused to be displaced. The town's most visible landmark is Mount Skopos.

Located near the village Argassi, Mount Skopos is 492m high and offers great views of Zakynthos. It is also the site of the Monastery of Panagia Skopiotissa, Zante's oldest church, which dates back to the 15th century. The church occupies the same spot as a former temple of Artemis and was constructed in the shape of a cross. The church features wall paintings of various saints as well as an icon representing the Panagia Skopiotissa. The Iconostasis is a feature common to most Orthodox churches, but at Panagia Skopiotissa or the Church of the Virgin Mary of Skopiotissa, it is constructed of stone, rather than the wood normally used.

🌎 Beaches

All the beaches on Zante are public, but with some access is controlled at certain times for ecological reasons. Gerakas Beach is located on the eastern side of the Laganas Bay area. As it forms part of the nesting ground of the loggerhead sea turtle, Caretta Caretta, no humans are allowed here between sundown and sunrise. Enjoying the daytime hours in the sun here might be well worth your while, and if the conditions are right and you are a strong swimmer, you may even be lucky enough to experience a close encounter with a loggerhead turtle in the water. Gerakas is considered one of the top beaches in Europe.

Collections of rock formations form an impressive backdrop to this golden beach and there is also a nearby clay canyon, which is similar to the 'Cappadocia' in Turkey. The natural beauty of the region is largely unspoilt by beachfront bars or water sport facilities. There are a few restaurants and snack bars a little way from the beach. Gerakas is 18km from Zante Town.

Another beach that forms part of the National Marine Park is Dafni beach. Here too, the loggerhead turtles enjoy legal protection and facilities are minimal to avoid disrupting their breeding cycle. The beach offers a rare view of the island, Pelouza, which is not accessible to visitors. Conditions at Dafni are favorable for swimming and snorkelling. Just off the Gerakas Peninsula, you will find Porto Roma, a small, peaceful beach favored by families. Another nearby beach is Porto Zoro.

At 9km, Laganas has the longest beach on the whole island of Zante. Its waters are shallow and pleasantly warm and the sand is delicate and fine. To protect the turtles that nest here in the summer months, no powered water sports or boats are allowed and access is restricted between sundown and sunrise. There are sun beds and umbrellas available for rental, as well as several beachside taverns.

The beautiful scenery of Porto Vromi includes picturesque coves and impressive rocks and cliffs. It is good for swimming and snorkelling, but also provides access via boat to the isolated Navagio or Shipwreck beach. Sometimes referred to as Smuggler's Cove, Navagio is Zante's most famous beach. Its shipwreck dates back to 1980. Once a smuggler's vessel carrying contraband tobacco and, it ran aground in stormy weather and is now a distinctive feature of this very recognizable area. The beach is only accessible from the sea. Its cliffs form a dramatic backdrop, but the water is quite cold, compared to that of most beaches of Zante.

🌐 Nightlife

One of the big draws to Zante is its nightlife. Laganas, the largest resort, is a Club 18-30 destination and draws a dedicated crowd of partygoers each summer. Its nightclubs employ world famous DJ's, sell an exotic selection of cocktails and offer attractions that can range from risqué to outrageous.

The Rescue Club (http://www.rescueclub.net) in Laganas can hold a crowd of over 2000 people. It is the only nightclub in Zante with that kind of capacity. It boasts 3 dance floors, 6 bars and an open-air VIP bar lounge. The Rescue Club has been operating since 1987 and attracts world-class DJs. It also hosts themed events such as a naughty back-to-school party and UV paint parties. Just remember not to wear your best and most expensive clothing to the latter, as it is likely to get covered in paint.

For fun pranks and bar games, do stop off at Zeros Club (http://www.zerosclubzante.com). Some of the events include a Foam Party, the suggestive Shag Tag nights and a Total Karnage bar crawl. The sound system is powerful and pumping, while the spectacular lighting may blow your expectations wide open. The multi-talented bartenders are part of the entertainment and roving club photographers may capture you at your best, or worst. Experience Laganas at its most outrageous at this venue.

Nightclubs worth a visit in Argassi are Barrage, with a chill-out garden section as well as a lively dance stage inside and the Factory Club, where the scene starts out fairly mellow in the late afternoon, but spices up towards the early hours of the morning. The Jungle Bar in Alykes offers a variety of liquid refreshments and music to suit a number of preferences. In the same town, you can dance the night away on the beach, when you visit Paraporo.

Visit the Level Bar in Tsilivi for exotic coffees, original cocktails and regular karaoke. Another Tsilivi nightspot, Kaliva also offers karaoke in the summer. It has a more family-friendly character, and includes a beautiful garden and play area. If you are looking for a real English bar, try Ozzy's and for a fusion of classic 60s, 70s and 80s favorites, visit Gyroland.

🌎 Scuba Diving

There is a great selection of fascinating diving sites concentrated on the Keri Peninsula. Of these, several have multi-faceted appeal. Some like Octopus Reef and Alati provide a good basic dive for the novice, but offer the challenge of additional features, for the more experienced diver. A guide will be able to structure your diving experience according to your proficiency level. Some of the Dive Centers that may be able to facilitate a tour of underwater exploration are Eurodivers

(http://eurodivers.nu/) in Laganas and the Turtle Beach

Diving Center (http://www.diving-center-turtle-beach.com/)

based in Limni Keriou.

At Octopus Reef, you can see grouper, moray eel and

bream. The limestone reef wall begins at 12m, and you

may discover not only marine life, but also a few artefacts

such as amphora vases from the past. Sections of this

site are more suitable to experienced divers. Barracuda

Reef features parrotfish, wrasse and loggerhead turtles,

but also larger predators such as blue fin turtles,

amberjack and grouper. Keri Caves presents a unique

challenge. Even above the water, the cliffs appear

spectacular, rising over 100m above the water. Below the

water, you will encounter a limestone reef with distinctive

boulders that attract a variety of marine life. Moving along this feature, you will eventually reach an enormous cave, marked with colorful corals and sponges. The cave system is recommended for more experienced divers.

The Arch, also known as Arc de Triumph is a diverse eco-system of limestone boulders colonised by corals, sponges, lobster, bream, parrotfish, octopus, grouper and moray eel. Descend a little lower, and you get to meet the larger predators. The site known as Two Columns comprises of a channel formed between the reef and the cliff itself. In places, it descends to a depth of 70m. The unique features of the cave at the White Reefs site will enable you to experience various shifts in tone and color. Another site that offers the unusual perception of underwater beauty, provided you are equipped with a torch, is Poseidon Cave. Other sites worth exploring include Dafni, Lakka, Marathonisi, Marathia, Elefant,

Pultas and Faros.

🌐 Askos Stone Park

Volimes

Tel: +30 26950 31650

http://www.askos.gr

The Askos Stone Park is located on the northern part of

the island, 1km from Volimes, 3km from Blue Caves and

30km from Zante Town. The name refers to a number of

old stone structures such as the remains of stable walls

and basins that can be found about the park. Nature,

however, is given free reign in this fascinating place.

The 170,000 plants found here, are largely self-sown and

the animals, which include raccoons, African goats,

peacocks and turtles, are maintained in habitats natural to their species. There are farm animals such as donkeys, ponies, cows and pigs, but also creatures of the wild, such as hawks. Some of the features include a vineyard, an olive grove, a cypress forest, a pigeon loft and a duck pond. There are various stone-carved water basins, one of which is around 600 years old. You can see ancient trees growing on rock or marvel at a stone structure used for winemaking. Devote some time to explore all of its fascinating features or to help out as a volunteer.

Budget Tips

🌐 Accommodation

Zante Star

Tsilivi

Tel: +30 26950 23495

http://www.zantestar.com

One testimony to Zante Star Hotel's service and

popularity is the fact that many of its guests are repeat visitors.

The hotel is located 5 to 10 minutes stroll from the beach on a hill surrounded by olive groves and it caters for all age groups with its activities and facilities. There is a restaurant and a bar/lounge area and the swimming pool has plenty of loungers and umbrellas. Staff members are described as friendly and helpful. Rooms include bathroom facilities with a hairdryer, a safe box and a well-equipped kitchenette.

The Prive apartments, which can sleep up to six people, include a television and more wardrobe space. Air-conditioning is charged separately, priced at about €45 per week. Accommodation begins at €16 per night.

Breakfast is not included in the price, but economically priced and great value for money.

Hotel Strada Marina

14 Lomvardou, Zakynthos Town

Tel: +30 26950 42761

http://www.stradamarina.gr

Hotel Strada Marina is located in the heart of Zante Town, and within walking distance of the ferry terminal, shops, restaurants and most of the city's tourist attractions. The hotel is wheelchair-friendly and has a rooftop garden, swimming pool and bar, which offers a lovely atmosphere and great views of the city. The decor is reminiscent of the eighties, but rooms are clean and well maintained. Rooms include individually controlled air-conditioning, satellite TV, a mini-bar, bathroom facilities and free high-speed Internet. A laundry service is included.

Accommodation begins at €60 and includes a Greek

buffet breakfast.

Cronulla Hotel

Kalamaki

Tel: +30 26950 45317

http://www.cronullahotel.com

Kalamaki is located near the airport and the popular

resort, Laganas, but somehow avoids the rowdy, over-

the-top character of the latter. The hotel is about 5 to 10

minutes walk away from the beach. It has a beautiful pool,

with sun beds to lounge around in all day. Rooms are

spacious and well maintained. All rooms include air-

conditioning, a fully equipped kitchen with fridge, kettle

and other utensils. Accommodation is €37 per night in the

off season and €50 in the high season, but you will be able to save a little by enquiring about weekly rates, if you plan a slightly longer stay.

Poseidon Beach Hotel

Laganas

Tel: +30 26950 51830

http://www.poseidon-zakynthos.gr

The Poseidon Beach Hotel is located a mere 50m away from the beach and about 500m from Laganas Town. It has a swimming pool with Jacuzzi and plenty of sun beds, a garden, a music beach bar and a snack bar. Free wireless Internet is available throughout the hotel. Rooms include air-conditioning, satellite TV, bathroom facilities, a refrigerator and a safe deposit box. Accommodation begins at €50 a night.

Contessa Hotel

Argassi

Tel: +30 26950 45585

http://www.contessahotel.gr

The Contessa is a family hotel located in Argassi that offers great views of both the mountains and the sea. A variety of entertainment options are available. There is a golf course nearby and the hotel has a swimming pool, a play area, DVDs, a billiards table and a beautiful roof garden. Management organizes social events such as a weekly barbeque. Rooms include air-conditioning, bathroom facilities, television, refrigerator, safe deposit box and Wi-Fi. Accommodation begins at €35 for the most basic unit and includes breakfast.

🌐 Places to Eat

Thymalos

78 Lombardou Street, Zante Town

Although located centrally within the tourist district of Zante Town, Thymalos is surprisingly affordable and features great seafood on their menu. The decor is rustic and friendly. Your meal should begin with a complimentary drink of raki and some bread.

Some of the menu highlights include Thailand shrimp, Fisherman's pasta, Octapus with honey and prawn saganaki. You can expect to pay between €12 and €14 per person for a selection of starters, a salad, a main dish and some wine. The meal will be rounded off by a small dessert that is on the house. An added bonus of

Thymalos is the free Wi-Fi.

Obelix Restaurant

Tsilivi

Obelix is a typical Greek taverna that offers good food,

speedy service and affordable prices. Some of the menu

items include mousaka, souvlaki, pork gyros, kleftiko,

stifado, lamb chops and steak. Seafood dishes such as

swordfish and calamari are expertly prepared. Try the

Greek Mixed Plate, which is great value for money or

come early and enjoy the English breakfast. Expect to pay

around €20 for a three course meal plus wine per person.

The Green Frog

Main Rd, Argassi

Tel: +30 26950 22596

http://www.thegreenfrogzante.com

The Green frog is a family restaurant that boasts a colorful and funky decor and offers food and entertainment for a wide variety of tastes.

Some of the attractions include karaoke, quiz nights, tribute acts and hypnotists. There are fun children's activities throughout the day and these include a bouncing castle, splash days and football. Breakfast, lunch and dinner is served and the menu offers a pleasant mix of Greek and international food. Some of the items include moussaka, calamari, club sandwiches, lamb and pork chops, Greek pita, oven-baked pizza, carbonara pasta, various salads and fish and chips. On the beverage side, there are a number of creative cocktails available. There are even options to share, such as the Greek Meze Platter. Expect to dine for around €10 or less.

Olive Tree

Main Rd, Kalamaki

Tel: +30 26950 49253

http://www.facebook.com/olivetreezante

At Olive Tree, one of the busiest restaurants in the Kalamaki beach area, it pays to be early for dinner. Between 5 and 8pm, patrons qualify for a free starter or dessert with their meal. There are a number of Greek favorites on the menu such as chicken souvlaki, moussaka, beef youvetsi and beef stifado, but there are also a few other variations, such as Mexican Chicken.

Further choices include vegetarian courgette fritters, lamb

skewer, chicken and beef fajitas and Greek plate.

Portions are generous and the service is attentive. Most

mains are priced around €7. An added bonus is the free

Wi-Fi. This restaurant should not be confused with The

Olive Tree in Tsilivi, which also comes highly

recommended.

Horizon Restaurant

Laganas Beach, Laganas

Tel: +30 26950 52791

http://www.horizonzante.gr

Horizon restaurant is aptly named, as it offers beautiful

sea views over the Laganas beach area. A visit to the

restaurant included free use of the sun beds of the beach,

but you may prefer to relax in the roof garden. Horizon

also offers Wi-Fi coverage and Greek dancing for

entertainment. The menu is a combination of Greek and

International food. Some of the highlights include Greek

lamb, T-bone steak and calamari. On the dessert side,

you may want to sample the homemade cheesecake or

the bannoffee pie. Expect to pay around €23 for starters,

a main meal, drinks and dessert for one person.

🌍 Shopping

Zante Pleasures

12 Lombardou Street, Zante Port

http://www.mantolato.gr

Part of the fun of visiting a foreign country is the pleasure

of sampling its delicacies. Zante Pleasures produces a

variety of home made sweets. Its speciality is nougat,

called mantolato, which is manufactured using egg whites, almonds and lots of honey.

Other products are pasteli, a bar made of seeds, nuts and honey, wine, honey, cheese and olive oil. Olive oil is one of the main export products of Zante and the local cheese is Ladotyri, a hard, spicy cheese made of sheep and goat's milk. Honey is produced locally in the higher regions. The factory also stocks local perfumes and some souvenirs.

The Mantolato Factory is located about 1km from Zante Town, in the village of Panagoula, but the factory has several sales outlets in Zante Town. Besides the one in Lombardou Street, there is also a shop at 12 El. Venizelou Street and one at the corner of T. Kefalinou and An Makri.

O Zakynthos

21 May St 14, Zante Town

Tel: +30 26950 44615

http://www.ozakynthos.gr

O Zakynthos sells the creative and sometimes quirky jewellery of a number of Greek designers based. The business was founded in 1981. The works include traditional elements such as gold, silver and precious stones, but also alternative materials and modern approaches to jewellery. The shop is located near St Marco Square in Zante Town.

Gold M

Tavoulari 2, Zante Town

Tel: +30 26950 23902

When it comes to buying jewellery in Zante, the Big M is widely sought after. This stands for Michalopoulos, the man behind the business that dates back to 1960. The shop carries a wide range of jewellery and is the only authorized agent on Zante for a number of well-known brands such as Swatch, Omega, Tag Heuer, Versace and Gucci. There is also a collection of silver jewellery and decorative items.

Buying Ceramics

Adamieion Ceramic Art Studio

Marineika

Tel: +30 26950 62400

http://www.adamieion.com

The Adamieion Ceramic Art Studio is located not far from Tsilivi, in the village of Marineika and features the art of

Dionysia Avouri, who was trained in Athens. The studio displays a mixture of functional and decorative ceramic items and incorporates a variety of themes.

This includes the Byzantine Blue collection, the Olive collection, the Metallic Gold collection, the Egyptian Green collection, the Crazy Fishes collection and the Sea Life collection. Besides plates, you will also find a creative range of tiles, dolls and other sculptures.

Hanne Mi

Vassilikos

Tel: +30 26950 35012

http://www.ceramichannemi.com

Hanne Mi is a Norwegian Ceramic artist who has settled in the Vassilikos area. She produces a variety of tiles, plates, bowls, cups and sculptures that are well formed and tastefully decorated. In the summer season, she also offers two-hour hands-on workshops where visitors can craft their own little souvenir for €20.

Andriani's Ceramic Workshop

Agios Sostis Village

Tel: +30 26950 52748

http://www.andrianiceramic.gr

Andriani sells a number of creative and colorful designs, including plates, cups and tiles. You can browse through the exhibition area and then take a closer look at the manufacturing process in the workshop. The studio is located in Agios Sostis Village, near Laganas.

Levantino Gift Shop

Kalamaki Main Rd, Kalamaki

Tel: +30 26950 22848

If you are looking for any kind of souvenir that says I've been to Zante, one suitable place to stop is the Levantino Gift Shop. Spread across three different floors, it stocks beach gear, such as bags, sandals and sunglasses, T-shirts, including special ones that feature the Caretta Caretta turtles, gold and silver jewellery, a variety of olive and olive oil products, including soap, crockery, ceramics and other handcrafts. There are outlets in Kalamaki and Laganas, but Levantino also has a branch in Zante Town.

Know Before You Go

🌐 Entry Requirements

By virtue of the Schengen agreement, travellers from other countries in the European Union do not need a visa when visiting Greece. Additionally visitors from certain countries such as Canada, Japan, Israel, Australia, Argentina, Monaco, Andorra, Brazil, Brunei, Chile, Costa Rica, Croatia, Honduras, Guatemala, El Salvador, Nicaragua, Paraguay, Panama, San Marino, Singapore, South Korea, Uruguay, New Zealand and the Vatican State do not need visas if their stay in Greece does not exceed 90 days in a six month period. In the case of travellers from the USA, entry requirements will depend on the type of passport held. While visitors with a normal blue tourist passport will be able to enter the USA without a visa, holders of red official or black diplomatic passports must apply for a Schengen visa prior to departure and will face deportation if attempting to enter Greece without the necessary documentation.

🌍 Health Insurance

Citizens of other EU countries as well as residents from Switzerland, Norway, Iceland, Liechtenstein and the UK are covered for health care in Greece with the European Health Insurance Card (EHIC), which can be applied for free of charge. If you need a Schengen visa for your stay in Greece, you will also be required to obtain proof of health insurance for the duration of your stay (that offers at least €37,500 coverage), as part of your visa application. Visitors from Canada or the USA should check whether their regular health insurance covers travel and arrange for extended health insurance if required.

🌍 Travelling with Pets

Greece participates in the Pet Travel Scheme (PETS) which allows UK residents to travel with their pets without requiring quarantine upon re-entry. Pets travelling between different countries in the EU will need to be accompanied by a valid pet passport, which can be obtained from any licensed veterinarian in the EU. The animal will have to be microchipped and up to date on rabies vaccinations. To visit Greece, your pet will need to be accompanied by a good health certificate issued by a vet no more than ten days prior to your intended departure. The certificate must be in both English and Greek. You should also have a rabies vaccination certificate no less than 30 days and no more than 12 months old. If travelling from a high rabies country, a blood titer test will need to be submitted three months prior to your travel plans. Your animal's microchip should be non-encrypted and compliant with a 15 digit ISO 11784/11785 number (or alternatively you will need to have your own scanner handy.) You will be required to make a declaration of non-commercial travel. If returning to the USA with a pet you adopted in Greece, your pet will need to be vaccinated against rabies at least 30 days prior to entry into the USA.

🌍 Airports

Athens International Airport (ATH) is the busiest airport in Greece. Located about 20km east of the city center, it is the main airport servicing Athens and the region of Attica. **Heraklion International Airport** (HER) is located on the island of Crete, about 5km east of the city of Heraklion. It is the second busiest airport in Greece. **Thessaloniki International Airport** (SKG), also known as Makedonia International Airport, provides access to Khalkidhiki, the region of Macedonia and the northern part of Greece. It is located in Mikra and serves Thessaloniki, the second largest city in Greece. **Rhodes International Airport** (RHO) is located on the western side of the island Rhodes. It is the 4th busiest airport in Greece, providing regular connections to Athens. **Corfu**

International Airport (CFU) is located on the island of Corfu, about 2km south of Corfu City. **Mykonos Island National Airport** (JMK) about 4km from Mykonos Town and **Santorini National Airport** (JTR), provide seasonal connections to the Cyclades at the peak of the summer holidays.

🌏 Airlines

Olympic Airlines, the national flag carrier of Greece for more than 50 years, ceased operation in 2009 due to bankruptcy. From the privatization of its assets, a regional airline, Olympic Air, was formed. Ellinair is a small Greek airline that was established in 2013 and provides regional connections between Athens and Thessaloniki as well as regular flights to Russia, Latvia and the Ukraine. Minoan Air is a small airline based in Heraklion on the island of Crete. It provides connections to Kos and Rhodes, as well as seasonal flights to Santorini and Mytilene. Sky Express is also headquartered in Crete and provides regional connections to 18 Greek destinations. Another Greek airline based in Crete, Bluebird Airways, flies to the Greek destinations of Araxos, Corfu, Kos and Rhodes as well as destinations in Israel, Russia and Turkey.

Athens International Airport serves as a main hub for Aegean Airlines as well as Olympic Air. Olympic Air also uses Rhodes International Airport as a secondary hub. Heraklion International Airport serves as a hub for Bluebird Airways

Minoan Air and Sky Express. It is also a focus city for Aegean Airlines. Thessaloniki International Airport serves as a hub for Aegean Airlines, Astra Airlines, Ellinair and Ryanair.

🌐 Currency

The currency of Greece is the Euro. It is issued in notes in denominations of €500, €200, €100, €50, €20, €10 and €5. Coins are issued in denominations of €2, €1, 50c, 20c, 10c, 5c, 2c and 1c.

🌐 Banking & ATMs

You will find ATMs in the larger centers of Greece, although smaller towns may only have a single ATM machine. Greek ATMs are configured for four-digit PIN numbers - make sure your card is compliant before leaving home. However, the financial crisis has introduced an added complication. While daily limits imposed on Greek citizens do not apply to tourists visiting the country, you may encounter ATMs that have run out of cash or banks that are reluctant to exchange pounds for euros. The limits imposed on Greeks will also make it difficult for shop owners to provide change for cash sales. To be on the safe side, consider taking cash in smaller denominations. Do remember to advise your bank of your travel plans before leaving home.

🌐 Credit Cards

The Credit Cards most widely used in Greece are MasterCard and Visa, although American Express is also accepted at more touristy centers. While shops and many hotels accept credit cards, most restaurant options will be limited to cash. Credit card machines in Greece are configured for chip-and-pin type credit cards and you may run into trouble with an older magnetic strip credit card. Greece also has representatives of Western Union, for international money transfers.

🌐 Reclaiming VAT

If you are not from the European Union, you can claim back VAT (Value Added Tax) paid on your purchases in Greece. The VAT rate in Greece is 23 percent, although it varies on certain types of goods and you will qualify for a refund on goods of €120 and over. To reclaim, you must ask the merchant to fill in a refund voucher. You will be asked to show your passport. Make sure that the form is completed and attach your sales slip to the form. The goods must be inspected at the place where you leave the European Union. Here, the necessary documentation will be processed. Your refund will only be valid for items that are still unused at your time of departure. If the merchant is affiliated to Global Refund or Premier Tax Free, you will be able to collect the refund from their offices at the airport in the currency of your choice. A 4 percent service charge will be levied. Alternatively, you could ask for a refund on your credit card or contact the retailer directly, once you have returned home.

🌍 Tipping Policy

At the hotel, tip the porter €1 per bag and the housekeeper €1 per day. At restaurants, you should tip between 5 and 10 percent of the bill, depending on its size. Bear in mind that the service or cover charge on your restaurant bill (usually around €1) is for the table's bread and water. It is customary to tip tour guides in Greece. For a group tour, between €2 and €5 per person is fair. For private tours, €20 per person is the expected rate. On a yacht cruise, tip the captain or skipper between 5 and 15 percent (in a closed envelope) for him to distribute amongst crew members. With taxi drivers, it is customary to round off the amount or to tip between 5 and 10 percent. If you employed a private driver, tip him €20 per day.

🌍 Mobile Phones

Most EU countries, including Greece uses the GSM mobile service. This means that most UK phones and some US and Canadian phones and mobile devices will work in Greece. However, phones using the CDMA network will not be compatible. While you could check with your service provider about coverage before you leave, using your own service in roaming mode will involve additional costs. The alternative is to purchase a Greek SIM card to use during your stay in Greece. Greece has three mobile networks. They are Cosmote, Vodafone and Wind. Of the three networks, Wind is the most economic, but offers the lowest coverage. With each network, you can choose between packages that offer data only or a mixture of voice, text and data. A basic Cosmote SIM with no credit can be purchased for €5, but you will want to look at some of the available package deals as well. Vodafone offers a starter package that includes 2 GB data that can be ordered online for €15, but will cost €20 in store. At Wind you have the choice of a free SIM with top-up cards from €10 or a SIM for €5. They also offer mobile broadband. As per legislation that came into effect in 2009, all Greek SIM cards must be registered before they can be activated. This can only be done in person and you will need to show some form of identification, such as a passport. You can recharge your airtime by buying scratch cards or electronically from ATMs, certain vendors or online with a debit or credit card.

🌐 Dialling Code

The international dialling code for Greece is +30.

Emergency numbers

General Emergencies: 112

Police: 100

Fire Brigade: 199

Emergency Medical Service: 166

Coast Guard: 108

Emergency Social Assistance: 197

Tourist Police: 171

MasterCard: 00 800 11 887 0303

Visa: 00 800 11 638 0304

Public Holidays

1 January: New Year's Day

6 January: Day of the Epiphany

February/March: Orthodox Ash Monday

25 March: Independence Day

April (variable): Orthodox Good Friday

April (variable): Orthodox Easter Sunday

April (variable): Orthodox Easter Monday

1 May: Labour Day

May/June: Orthodox Pentecost

May/June: Orthodox Whit Monday

15 August: Assumption Day

28 October: Ochi Day (Oxi Day/Ohi Day)

25 December: Christmas Day

26 December: Second Christmas Day

🌍 Time Zone

Greece falls in the Eastern European Time Zone. This can be calculated (from the end of October to the end of March) as follows: Greenwich Mean Time/Coordinated Universal Time (GMT/UTC) +2; Eastern Standard Time (North America) -6; Pacific Standard Time (North America) -9.

🌍 Daylight Savings Time

Clocks are set forward one hour on the last Sunday of March and set back one hour on the last Sunday of October for Daylight Savings Time.

🌍 School Holidays

The academic year begins in the second week of September and ends in mid June. The summer holiday is from mid June to the first third of September. There are short breaks between Christmas and New Year and also around Easter.

● Trading Hours

In Greece, trading hours vary according to the type of business. You can expect supermarkets to be open from 8am to 8pm on weekdays and until 6pm on Saturdays. Most other shops are open between 9am and 1pm and then again for a late session between 6pm and 9pm. The hours from 1.30pm to 5.30pm are for lunch and siesta, especially in the summer months. Post Offices are open from 8am to 8pm on weekdays and from 8am to 2pm on Saturdays. Shops that cater for tourists may be open until 11pm, especially during the peak tourist season. Pharmacies conform to normal shopping hours, but are usually closed on Saturdays.

● Driving Laws

Greeks drive on the right hand side of the road. A driver's licence from any of the European Union member countries is valid in Greece, but visitors from non-EU countries should apply for an International Driver's License. The minimum driving age in Greece is 18. You will need to have a Green Insurance certificate, also known as a Green Card to cover third party liability and your vehicle needs standard safety gear such as warning triangles, a first aid kit and fire extinguisher. Your vehicle also needs to have headlamp deflectors. The speed limit in Greece is 130km per hour on freeways and 50km an hour on urban roads. The alcohol limit in Greece is under 0.5 g/l. Children under the age of 10 are not allowed to ride in the front seat. It is illegal to use your mobile phone while driving.

Smoking Laws

Greece is the European country with the highest tobacco consumption rate. As a result, the population has been very tolerant of smoking, even with the introduction of anti-smoking legislation. In fact, business owners have appealed against various forms of anti-smoking laws, arguing that they are bad for business. Smoking in public places has been banned since 2010, but the law provides for bars, taverns, casinos, night clubs and betting shops to create a designated smoking area. It is also illegal to smoke in your car, if in the company of a minor child.

Drinking Laws

The legal drinking age in Greece is 18. Although Greece has a culture of social drinking, bars and night clubs may state that alcohol will not be served to under 18s or even, in the case of certain cruise tours, under 21s. Alcohol can be bought from supermarkets and even fast food outlets.

🌐 Electricity

Electricity: 230 volts

Frequency: 50 Hz

Greek electricity sockets use the Type F plugs, which feature two round pins or prongs. They are also compatible with Type C and Type E plugs. If travelling from the USA, you will need a power converter or transformer to convert the voltage from 230 to 110, to avoid damage to your appliances. The latest models of many laptops, camcorders, mobile phones and digital cameras are dual-voltage with a built in converter.

🌐 Tourist Information (TI)

There are three National Tourist Offices in the city of Athens where you can pick up maps of the city, as well as time tables for the Greek bus, train and ferry services. They are located at Athens Eleftherios Venizelos Airport, in the Athens Center at 26A Amalias Avenue and 7 Tsoha Street.

🌐 Food & Drink

Greek cuisine relies heavily on the use of olive oil (and olives), cheese and aubergines (or eggplant). Beef is rare, but there are plenty of lamb and pork dishes to make up for it. One of the most popular Greek dishes is moussaka, a casserole consisting of layers of eggplant and spiced mince. Try the baked pasta dish, pastitsio or if you like meat stews, do make sure that you try stifado as well. With an abundance of seafood available, don't forget to enjoy the abundance of grilled fish and octopus. A course of small meze dishes is often served as appetizer or to accompany a round of drinks. The standard meze favorites include tzatziki (a dip of yoghurt and cucumber), hummus (made of chickpea), dolmades, keftedes, olives, feta cheese and taramasalata (a fish roe dip), usually served with pita or flatbread. Another delicious appetizer is saganaki, or fried cheese, often made with halloumi, kefalotyri, graviera, kefalograviera or feta. Graviera, which is a native product of Crete, is the second most popular cheese in Greece after feta. Fast and meaty snacks to enjoy on the go are souvlaki (meat skewers), kebabs or gyros - pitas filed with meat, French fries and smothered in tzatziki. Phyllo pastry is used for a variety of dishes, including the standard dessert of baklava and tiropitakia (or cheese pies). If you happen to find yourself on Mykonos, do make sure you sample kopanisti, a cheesy appetizer, a few slices of louza, the local salami and some amigthalota, to indulge your sweet tooth. Crete is a must for cheese lovers, where practically every village has its own distinctive varieties. Here you can also enjoy Askordoulakous or "mountain bulbs", lamb with stamnagathi or sfakia pies. For a taste of manouri - a cheese similar to feta with a creamier character - you need to be in Thessaly or Macedonia.

The most popular beers local beer in Greece is Mythos, although Amstel and Heineken are also available at most venues. Retsina is the type of wine most often associated with Greece, although its distinctive taste of resin is not all that popular with foreigners. Another popular drink is ouzo, a strong liquor with a minty taste that combines well with seafood. If visiting Epirus, Macedonia or Crete, to sample the local raki and tsipouro, which is served in small shot glasses. If you want to quench your thirst with something refreshing and non-alcoholic, try soumada, a Cretan beverage of almond and rose water.

Websites

http://www.visitgreece.gr/

http://www.greeka.com/best-greece-destinations.htm

http://www.greek-tourism.gr/

http://wikitravel.org/en/Greece

http://www.visit-ancient-greece.com/

http://www.greektravel.com/mainland.htm

Printed in Great Britain
by Amazon